LE CORDON BLEU

HOME COLLECTION

BREAKFASTS

MURDOCH BOOKS®

Sydney • London • Vancouver • New York

D1122610

contents

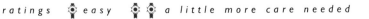

recipe ratings ❋ *easy* ❋❋ *a little more care needed* ❋❋❋ *more care needed*

Fresh fruit kebabs

Sweet fruit kebabs served hot with a little crème fraîche or yoghurt make a delicious alternative to fresh fruit salad.

*Preparation time **20 minutes + at least 2 hours standing + 30 minutes marinating***
*Total cooking time **7 minutes***
Serves 4

1 teaspoon finely chopped fresh rosemary
125 g (4 oz) clear honey
450 g (14¹/4 oz) mixed fruit, such as strawberries, kiwi fruit, mango, apricots or pineapple
2 teaspoons caster sugar

1 Combine the rosemary and honey with 2 tablespoons water in a saucepan and bring slowly to the boil over low heat. Remove, cool, cover with plastic wrap and leave for 2 hours or preferably overnight in the refrigerator.
2 Soak 16 small wooden skewers, or long ones cut to 15 cm (6 inch) lengths, in water for at least 30 minutes. Prepare the fruit by washing and peeling as appropriate. Leave fruit such as strawberries whole, cut kiwi fruit into thick slices, mango into large chunks, halve the apricots, and so on. The fruit should roughly match in size. Thread onto the skewers, place in a shallow dish and pour the honey and rosemary over the top. Set aside for 30 minutes, brushing the kebabs occasionally with the liquid.
3 Preheat the grill to high. Drain the fruit, reserving the liquid. Sprinkle the sugar on the fruit and grill in a shallow heatproof dish, in batches. Cook for 5–7 minutes, or until the edges are beginning to colour, brushing the fruit with the honey mixture halfway through cooking. Serve hot, drizzled with the juice, and with some crème fraîche on the side, if desired.

Chef's tip Dried fruit can be used. Combine in a pan with the prepared honey and rosemary, heat for 2 minutes, cool and thread onto skewers. Grill for 3 minutes.

Swiss muesli

A light, healthy start to the day, muesli may be made using a variety of fruits and nuts according to what is readily available.

*Preparation time **10 minutes***
*Total cooking time **10 minutes***
Serves 1

1 tablespoon raisins
150 g (5 oz) thick natural yoghurt
1 tablespoon clear honey
3 tablespoons rolled oats
2 tablespoons almonds or hazelnuts, toasted, skinned and chopped
1 passion fruit
1 small mango, cubed, or 1 banana, sliced, reserving a few pieces for decoration
a few extra toasted almonds, to garnish

1 Put the raisins in a small bowl, pour on boiling water to cover and set aside while preparing the muesli.
2 In a small bowl, stir the yoghurt, honey, rolled oats and nuts together.
3 With a small sharp knife, halve the passion fruit. Using a teaspoon, scoop out the seeds and pulp and add to the yoghurt mixture. Drain the raisins and add them to the mixture with the mango or banana. Mix gently until just combined.
4 Spoon into a bowl and decorate with the reserved fruit and the almonds.

Chef's tips If you like a sweeter muesli, drizzle with a little extra honey or demerara sugar before eating.

Fresh fruits of the season such as strawberries, peaches, pears or any others of your choice can also be used.

Fresh fruit kebabs (top) and Swiss muesli

Grilled grapefruit

How luxurious to be presented with a perfectly prepared grapefruit! Refreshing and tangy, these make an interesting starter for breakfast or brunch.

Preparation time **20 minutes**
Total cooking time **5 minutes**
Serves 4

2 large grapefruit, preferably pink
2 teaspoons Cointreau
I tablespoon demerara sugar
pinch of nutmeg

1 Halve the grapefruit through the equator and cut a thin sliver from the base of each so that each half will sit without tipping over. Using the point of a grapefruit knife, cut down each side of every membrane to loosen the segments. Be careful not to cut through the skin.
2 Still using the grapefruit knife, loosen the fruit from the sides and the base by cutting round where the flesh meets the white pith. If you want an even better result, remove the membrane by gently holding the segments down with the knife and pulling the membrane up towards the centre. Take hold of it and carefully pull it out with the central pithy core, leaving the segments neatly in position.
3 Tip out any excess juice and place the grapefruit on a heatproof tray or grill pan. Pour 1/2 teaspoon Cointreau on each half of grapefruit. Preheat the grill to a high temperature. Mix the sugar with the nutmeg and sprinkle over the grapefruit. Immediately place the grapefruit under the grill to heat through and lightly brown the surface. Serve hot on warm plates.

Chef's tip Steps 1 and 2 may be done the day before. Cover the grapefruit halves and refrigerate overnight.

Scrambled eggs with smoked salmon

Scrambled eggs are delicious served with toast, as a filling for croissants, or alternatively, in puff pastry cases. The key to making really creamy scrambled eggs is not to overcook them.

Preparation time **10 minutes**
Total cooking time **5 minutes**
Serves 4–6

125 g (4 oz) smoked salmon
10 eggs
80 ml (2³/4 oz) thick (double) cream
20 g (³/4 oz) unsalted butter
sprigs of fresh flat-leaf parsley, to garnish

1 Set aside a few whole pieces of smoked salmon for decoration. Finely chop the rest and set aside.
2 In a bowl, whisk the eggs with the cream and season with salt and pepper.
3 Melt the butter in a frying pan. Add the eggs and cook over medium heat, stirring constantly, for about 3–5 minutes, or until the eggs are thick and creamy but still have a flowing consistency. Stir in the chopped salmon and serve immediately, garnished with the whole pieces of salmon and some parsley. Serve with fingers of toast.

Chef's tips Scrambled eggs will continue cooking even when the pan is removed from the stove, so it is important that everything is ready to serve as soon as the eggs are done.

If you prefer, you can leave the salmon in whole pieces and serve it beside the eggs.

This combination also makes a delicious filling for warm fresh croissants.

Grilled grapefruit (top) and
Scrambled eggs with smoked salmon

French toast with berry compote

Enjoy this berry compote all year round as it may be made with fresh or frozen berries. Any leftover compote may be used to flavour plain yoghurt.

Preparation time **10 minutes**
Total cooking time **35 minutes**
Serves **4**

90 g (3 oz) sugar
juice of 1 lemon
500 g (1 lb) fresh or frozen strawberries, blueberries, raspberries, blackberries or cherries
90 g (3 oz) clear honey
6 eggs
90 ml (3 fl oz) thick (double) cream
pinch of ground cinnamon
80 g (2¾ oz) unsalted butter
8 slices of white bread
2 tablespoons icing sugar

1 Combine the sugar and the lemon juice with 3 tablespoons water in a saucepan. Heat until the sugar is dissolved. Stir in the fruit, bring to the boil, reduce the heat and simmer for 5–10 minutes, or until the fruit is soft but still whole. If using frozen fruit, use from frozen and cook it a little longer.

2 Strain the fruit and put the juice in a small pan with the honey. Bring to the boil, stirring well. Cook for 7–10 minutes, or until the juice coats the back of a spoon. Put the fruit in a bowl and stir the juice into the fruit.

3 In a bowl, whisk together the eggs, cream and cinnamon. Melt a quarter of the butter in a non-stick frying pan over medium heat. Dip two slices of bread in the egg and cook for 2–4 minutes, or until golden on both sides. Repeat with the remaining butter and bread, keeping the cooked slices in a warm oven. Put two slices of the French toast on each plate, dust with sifted icing sugar and serve with the fruit compote.

Eggs Benedict

Toasted English muffins topped with grilled bacon, lightly poached eggs and smothered in rich buttery hollandaise sauce. This American speciality is a truly memorable breakfast or brunch treat.

Preparation time **25 minutes**
Total cooking time **10 minutes**
Serves 4

HOLLANDAISE SAUCE
2 egg yolks
2 tablespoons water
90 g (3 oz) clarified butter (see Chef's tip), melted
1/2 teaspoon lemon juice

8 rashers bacon, rind removed
4 English muffins
3 tablespoons vinegar
8 eggs
**4 pitted black olives, cut in half, or
    8 slices of truffle**

1 To make the hollandaise sauce, follow the method in the Chef's techniques on page 63. Cover the surface with a disc of baking paper and keep warm over the hot water, off the heat.

2 Grill the bacon until crisp and toast the muffins. Put the bacon on the muffins and keep them warm.
3 To make the poached eggs, fill a large shallow pan with water and bring to the boil. Reduce the temperature to low and add the vinegar. The water should be barely simmering.
4 Crack the eggs one at a time into a small cup or bowl and carefully slide them into the vinegared water two or three at a time. Cook for 2–3 minutes, or until the egg white is firm but not hard. Very gently remove the eggs, using a slotted spoon, and drain well.
5 Immediately top each muffin and bacon with a poached egg. Cover with the hollandaise sauce, decorate with the olive halves and serve.

Chef's tip You will need 170 g (51/2 oz) butter to yield 90 g (3 oz) clarified butter. Melt the butter gently over low heat in a small heavy-based pan, without stirring or shaking the pan. Skim the froth from the top, then carefully pour the clear butter into another container, leaving the white sediment in the base of the pan. Cover and keep in the refrigerator for up to 4 weeks.

Rösti with bacon

This recipe enables you to use potatoes that have already been cooked, making a quick and delicious dish.

Preparation time **15 minutes**
Total cooking time **45 minutes**
Serves 6

500 g (1 lb) large, waxy potatoes
4 thin rashers bacon, rind removed
2 tablespoons oil
25 g (3/4 oz) unsalted butter
1 onion, thinly sliced

1 Preheat the oven to moderate 180°C (350°F/Gas 4). Scrub the unpeeled potatoes and put them in a saucepan. Cover with cold water, add salt, and bring to the boil. Reduce the heat and simmer for 10 minutes. Drain and leave the potatoes to cool completely. Meanwhile, fry the bacon in a hot dry pan or grill until crisp. Remove and chop or break into bite-sized pieces.
2 Peel the potatoes and either cut into fine sticks or coarsely grate them into a bowl. Add the bacon. In a large non-stick frying pan, heat 1 tablespoon oil and add the butter. Gently cook the onion until soft and transparent. Add to the potato and bacon, season with salt and pepper and mix for a few minutes.
3 To make individual rösti, spoon the mixture into ring moulds set on the base of the lightly oiled onion pan or into blini pans (one-portion frying pans). Press down with the back of a spoon or spatula. Brown the first side over medium heat for 5–7 minutes. Turn each rösti over, using a spatula, and put them back in the pan brown-side-up, being careful not to break up the potato. Cook the rösti for another 5 minutes, to crisp the bottom.
4 To make one large rösti, put the mixture into a large non-stick ovenproof frying pan with 1/2 tablespoon oil and brown the underneath over high heat. Transfer the pan to the oven for 15 minutes. Remove, then flip the rösti by turning it out onto a plate and carefully sliding it back into the pan. Add the remaining oil to the pan if necessary. Return the pan to the oven for 10 minutes. Turn the rösti out onto a plate and serve whole or cut into slices.

Chef's tip If you prefer plain rösti, leave out the bacon and serve with rashers of crispy bacon on the side.

Salmon kedgeree

An old favourite with a twist: salmon and dill replace the traditional smoked haddock. Prepare the ingredients the day before.

*Preparation time **20 minutes***
*Total cooking time **16 minutes***
Serves 4

2 eggs, at room temperature
50 g (1³/4 oz) unsalted butter
375 g (12 oz) salmon fillet, cooked and flaked
250 g (8 oz) long-grain rice, cooked and well drained
1 egg, beaten
3 tablespoons cream
1–2 teaspoons chopped fresh dill or snipped
  fresh chives

1 Bring a small pan of water to the boil, gently put in the two eggs, return to the boil and simmer for 7 minutes. Remove with a spoon and place in a bowl of iced water to cool. Tap the shells with the back of a spoon to craze them, then peel. Roughly chop the eggs on a plate. The yolks should still be a little moist.
2 Melt the butter in a frying pan, add the salmon and heat for 30 seconds. Add the rice and the chopped egg and, using a fish slice, toss over high heat for 2 minutes, or until hot. Keep your movements light and the mixture loose; you do not want to compact the rice.
3 Add the beaten egg with the cream. Continue to toss for 3–5 minutes, scraping the base of the pan, until the egg has set. Season, to taste. Pile onto a warm serving dish and scatter with the fresh dill or chives to serve.

Chef's tips For the best result, the rice needs to be as dry as possible, so cook it the day before, drain it well, cover and refrigerate.

Don't worry that the boiled eggs initially seem underdone as they will continue to cook in the kedgeree.

Basic pancakes

Thin, lacy pancakes made using this traditional batter may be cooked in advance and kept overnight in the refrigerator or frozen for later use.

Preparation time **5 minutes + 30 minutes resting**
Total cooking time **40 minutes**
Makes 12

100 g (3¹/4 oz) plain flour
¹/2 teaspoon salt
3 eggs, lightly beaten
I egg yolk
175 ml (5³/4 fl oz) milk
25 ml (³/4 fl oz) oil or melted clarified butter

1 Sift the flour and salt into a bowl. Make a well in the centre, drop in the eggs and yolk and mix with a wooden spoon or whisk, drawing in a little at a time. Combine the milk with 75 ml (2¹/2 fl oz) water and gradually add until all the flour is incorporated. Beat in the oil or butter until smooth. Cover and rest at room temperature for 30 minutes.
2 Melt a little oil or clarified butter in a shallow, heavy-based or non-stick pan, 19 cm (7¹/2 inches) in diameter, until almost smoking, then pour off any excess. This will leave a fine coating—enough to cook one pancake. From a jug or ladle, pour in a small amount of batter, swirling the pan to coat just the bottom with a thin layer. Cook for 1–2 minutes, or until the edges are brown. Loosen around the edge with a round-bladed knife and turn or flip the pancake and cook for another 1–2 minutes. Tip onto greaseproof or baking paper. Repeat with the remaining batter. Stack the pancakes with a piece of greaseproof paper between each, then cover to prevent drying out. Serve with lemon juice and sugar.

Chef's tip To store, stack the pancakes and wrap in foil. Seal in a plastic bag to refrigerate overnight or freeze for up to 3 months. Defrost in the refrigerator overnight.

Pancakes jubilee

Thin light pancakes rolled around a black cherry filling enhanced with lemon, cinnamon and Kirsch.

Preparation time **10 minutes**
Total cooking time **10 minutes**
Serves 6–8

I quantity basic pancakes
2 x 425 g (13¹/2 oz) cans pitted black cherries
finely grated rind of I lemon
I cinnamon stick or ¹/4 teaspoon ground cinnamon
I tablespoon cornflour
50 g (1³/4 oz) icing sugar
I tablespoon Kirsch
30 g (I oz) unsalted butter, melted
icing sugar, to dust

1 To prepare the filling, drain the cherries and pour the juice into a small pan. Add the lemon rind and cinnamon and slowly bring to the boil. Remove from the heat. In a bowl, mix the cornflour with a little water to make a paste and pour on half the hot juice. Blend well, stir it in to the juice in the pan, return the pan to the heat and stir until boiling. Reduce the heat, remove the cinnamon stick, add the cherries, icing sugar and Kirsch, and heat gently until the cherries are just warmed through.
2 Preheat the oven to warm 160°C (315°F/Gas 2–3). Spoon some of the cherry mixture into the centre of each pancake and roll up like a cigar. Place in an ovenproof dish in a single layer, brush with the melted butter and heat through in the oven for 5 minutes. Dust with sifted icing sugar and serve.

Chef's tip The filling for these crêpes can be varied. Chopped apricot or peach can be used instead of the cherries, and you can use amaretto instead of Kirsch. If the pancakes have been prepared in advance and are still chilled, reheat for 10 minutes, covered with foil.

Basic pancakes (bottom) and Pancakes jubilee

Brunch pancake stack

This stack can be prepared the day before. The egg white, however, must be whisked and folded in at the last moment. Experiment by creating your own fillings for the layers or even using up leftovers.

Preparation time **25 minutes**
Total cooking time **1 hour 45 minutes**
Serves **4–6**

TOMATO FILLING
30 g (1 oz) unsalted butter
1 French shallot, finely chopped
1 teaspoon paprika
2 teaspoons tomato paste
1 kg (2 lb) tomatoes, halved, seeded and roughly chopped
small pinch of sugar

MUSHROOM FILLING
30 g (1 oz) unsalted butter
1 French shallot, finely chopped
120 g (4 oz) flat mushrooms, chopped
1 teaspoon plain flour
3 tablespoons milk
1 tablespoon chopped fresh parsley
small pinch of ground nutmeg

HAM FILLING
90 g (3 oz) ham, finely chopped (or chopped cooked bacon, sausages or chicken)
1 teaspoon French mustard
1 tablespoon chutney

20 g (3/4 oz) unsalted butter
3 teaspoons plain flour
220 ml (7 fl oz) milk
1 egg, separated
45 g (1 1/2 oz) strong Cheddar, grated
1 tablespoon grated Parmesan
7 thin pancakes (see page 16)

1 To prepare the tomato filling, melt the butter in a pan, add the shallot, cover and cook for 4–5 minutes, or until transparent. Stir in the paprika for 1 minute, add the tomato paste and stir over low heat for another minute. Add the tomato and sugar, season, and simmer for about 45 minutes, or until thick. Cover and set aside.

2 To make the mushroom filling, melt the butter in a pan, add the shallot, cover and cook for 4–5 minutes, or until transparent. Add the mushrooms and cook until dry. Remove from the heat and stir in the flour and milk. Return to a low heat and stir continuously until the liquid is smooth and begins to thicken. Increase the heat and stir as the mixture comes to the boil. Simmer for 1 minute, remove from the stove and stir in the parsley, nutmeg, salt and pepper. Cover and set aside.

3 To prepare the ham filling, mix together all the ingredients in a small bowl. Set aside.

4 Melt the butter in a pan, add the flour off the heat and stir for 1 minute. Pour in the milk, whisk to blend and return to the stove over low heat. Stir continuously until the mixture is smooth and begins to thicken, then increase the heat and bring to the boil. Remove from the stove. Stir in the egg yolk and half the Cheddar and Parmesan. Season, cover and set side.

5 Preheat the oven to moderately hot 200°C (400°F/ Gas 6). Butter a round ovenproof plate or pie dish about 25–28 cm (10–11 inches) across the base. Put a pancake on the base and spread with half the ham filling. Cover with another pancake and spread with half the mushroom filling, cover with a third pancake and spoon over half the tomato filling. Repeat with the rest of the pancakes and filling. Top with a final pancake, brownest-side-up.

6 To finish, whisk the egg white and fold it into the sauce. Spoon over the stack (a little may go over the edge) sprinkle with the remaining cheese and bake for 15 minutes, or until golden. Cut into six portions.

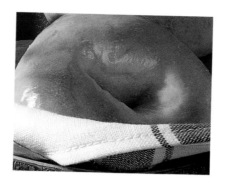

Bagels

Whether plain or sprinkled with sesame or poppy seeds, these yeasted bread rolls, characteristic of Jewish baking, are delicious served warm with butter. The traditional shiny, hard crust is achieved by boiling the bagels before baking them. See page 63 for step-by-step instructions to accompany this recipe.

*Preparation time **50 minutes + 1 hour proving***
*Total cooking time **25 minutes***
Makes 12 large or 24 small bagels

30 g (1 oz) fresh yeast or 15 g (¹/₂ oz) dried yeast
2 tablespoons oil
2 teaspoons salt
50 g (1³/₄ oz) caster sugar
500 g (1 lb) strong or plain flour
1 egg, beaten, for glazing

1 Dissolve the yeast in 250 ml (8 fl oz) lukewarm water, then add the oil.
2 Combine the salt, sugar and flour, then make a well in the centre. Add the yeast mixture and gradually incorporate the flour until a dough forms. Continue working the dough until the sides of the bowl come clean. Knead the dough for 10 minutes, then form it into a ball and place in the bottom of the bowl.

Cover with a moist towel and set aside in a warm place to rise for about 30–45 minutes, or until double in size. Line two baking trays with baking paper.
3 Once the dough has doubled in size, punch it down and knead for 8–10 minutes, then divide into 12 or 24 pieces. Roll them into tight balls. Poke a finger through the centre and gently enlarge the hole until the dough resembles a doughnut. Place on a floured baking tray, cover with a moist towel and allow to rise a second time for 15 minutes. Preheat the oven to moderately hot 200°C (400°F/Gas 6).
4 In the meantime, bring a pan of water to a simmer. Cook the bagels in the water for 1 minute on each side, then remove and place on the lined baking trays. Allow to cool for 5 minutes. Brush each bagel with beaten egg and bake for 20–25 minutes, or until golden brown.

Chef's tip Once the bagels have been brushed with the egg, they can be sprinkled with poppy seeds or sesame seeds before baking.

Eggs en cocotte with smoked trout and leek

Eggs that are 'en cocotte' are baked in the oven in ramekins placed in a bain-marie. An excellent breakfast dish, these eggs would also make a wonderful first course.

*Preparation time **15 minutes***
*Total cooking time **35 minutes***
Serves 4

30 g (1 oz) unsalted butter
1 small leek, halved and finely sliced
185 g (6 oz) smoked trout, flaked finely
120 ml (4 fl oz) cream
4 eggs
3 teaspoons snipped fresh chives

1 Melt the butter in a saucepan. Add the leek, cover and cook gently for 8 minutes, or until soft but not brown. Meanwhile, brush four 8.5 x 4 cm (3¹/4 x 1¹/2 inches), 150 ml (5 fl oz) capacity ovenproof ramekins or soufflé dishes with a little melted butter.

2 Remove the leek from the heat and stir in the trout and a third of the cream. Season, spoon into the dishes and leave to cool. The cocottes can be prepared up to this stage the night before, covered and refrigerated.

3 Preheat the oven to warm 170°C (325°F/Gas 3). With the back of a teaspoon, make a slight indent in the centre of the mixture in each of the dishes. Break an egg into each cocotte, spoon a tablespoon of cream on each and sprinkle with salt and pepper and 2 teaspoons of the chives. Place the dishes in a roasting tin and pour in enough boiling water to come halfway up the sides.

4 Bake for 20–25 minutes, or until the white is set and the yolk is cooked but still trembles when lightly shaken. Set each cocotte on a cold plate, sprinkle with the remaining chives and serve immediately with fingers of freshly made buttered toast.

Frittata

Unlike a French omelette, the Italian frittata usually requires all ingredients to be mixed with the eggs before being cooked to a fairly firm texture.

*Preparation time **20 minutes***
*Total cooking time **30 minutes***
Serves 4–6

120 g (4 oz) skinless chicken breast fillet
60 g (2 oz) unsalted butter
120 g (4 oz) mushrooms, sliced
2 cloves garlic, chopped
1 red capsicum (pepper), sliced into short strips
10 eggs, beaten and seasoned with salt and pepper
120 g (4 oz) Gruyère or Cheddar, grated

1 Preheat the oven to hot 220°C (425°F/Gas 7).

2 Cut the chicken breast into small 1 cm (1/2 inch) cubes and season with salt and pepper. Melt the butter in an ovenproof frying pan over medium heat. Once the butter has melted, cook the chicken for 2–3 minutes, until lightly browned.

3 Add the mushrooms and cook for 5–7 minutes, or until any liquid has evaporated. Add the garlic and red capsicum. Season with salt and pepper and cover. Lower the heat and cook gently for 5–8 minutes, or until the capsicum is tender.

4 Add the beaten eggs and stir to distribute evenly. Continue stirring for about 2–3 minutes, or until the eggs begin to set.

5 Sprinkle the cheese over the eggs and transfer the frying pan to the oven. Cook for 5–8 minutes, or until the cheese has melted and the eggs are cooked through. Remove from the oven and slide the frittata onto a plate. Cut into wedges to serve.

Eggs en cocotte with smoked trout and leek (top) and Frittata

Coffee granita with panna cotta

A coffee-flavoured granita teamed with a silky Italian custard makes a refreshing start to the day.

Preparation time **1 hour + overnight chilling**
Total cooking time **20 minutes**
Serves 4

235 g (7¹/4 oz) caster sugar
15 g (¹/2 oz) instant dark roast coffee powder
30 ml (1 fl oz) coffee liqueur, optional
4 leaves gelatine or 2 teaspoons powdered gelatine
2 vanilla pods, split lengthways
250 ml (8 fl oz) milk
250 ml (8 fl oz) thick (double) cream

1 Simmer 175 ml (5³/4 fl oz) water and 175 g (5³/4 oz) of the sugar in a pan for 10 minutes. Mix the coffee with a little water to form a paste and stir in. Leave to cool.
2 Add 500 ml (16 fl oz) water and the liqueur. Pour the granita into a shallow plastic or metal container and freeze overnight.
3 Soak the gelatine leaves in enough water to cover, adding each leaf separately, or dissolve the powder in 2 tablespoons hot water. Scrape the vanilla seeds into a pan and add the pods, milk, cream and remaining sugar. Bring to the boil, strain into a bowl and discard the pods.
4 Add the gelatine to the hot milk mixture (if you are using leaves, squeeze out any excess water first), then stir to melt. Place the bowl inside a bowl of ice water and stir until the gelatine begins to set (as the spoon is drawn through it, you will see a line across the base of the bowl). Pour into four 100 ml (3¹/4 fl oz) capacity moulds or ramekins. Chill overnight.
5 Half an hour before serving, refrigerate four plates. Release the panna cotta from the moulds by wrapping in a hot cloth and turning over. Scoop out the granita in flakes by drawing the side of a metal spoon across its surface. Serve on the chilled plates with the panna cotta.

Caramelized onion, spinach and blue cheese quiche

*The delicious combination of vegetables with blue cheese and a hint of nutmeg
makes a perfect filling for this vegetarian quiche.*

Preparation time **30 minutes + 50 minutes refrigeration**
Total cooking time **1 hour 45 minutes**
Serves 8–10

PASTRY
200 g (6¹/2 oz) plain flour
I teaspoon salt
100 g (3¹/4 oz) unsalted butter, chilled and cubed
I egg, lightly beaten

FILLING
2 tablespoons vegetable oil
500 g (I lb) onions, thinly sliced
I teaspoon caster sugar
100 ml (3¹/4 fl oz) red wine
50 g (1³/4 oz) unsalted butter
250 g (8 oz) frozen spinach, thawed and squeezed dry
pinch of ground nutmeg
200 ml (6¹/2 fl oz) thick (double) cream
**200 g (6¹/2 oz) strong blue cheese, such as Roquefort
  or Stilton**
4 eggs, beaten

1 Brush a 24 x 3.5 cm (9¹/2 x 1¹/4 inch) loose-bottomed flan tin with melted butter. Sieve together the flour and salt into a large bowl, add the butter and, using a fast, light flicking action of the thumb across the tips of the fingers, rub into the flour until the mixture resembles fine breadcrumbs. Make a well in the centre and pour in the egg and 2 teaspoons water. Bring together to a rough ball. Turn out onto a lightly floured surface and knead very gently for 20 seconds until just smooth, place in plastic wrap and chill for at least 20 minutes.
2 Roll out the pastry on a floured surface to a circle approximately 3 mm (¹/8 inch) thick. Fold half the pastry over the rolling pin and lift into the tin. Push into the sides of the tin by using a small ball of lightly floured excess pastry. Trim off any excess pastry with a sharp knife or roll over the top of the tin with the rolling pin. Refrigerate for 30 minutes. Preheat the oven to moderate 180°C (350°F/Gas 4).
3 Cut a circle of greaseproof paper 3 cm (1¹/4 inches) larger than the flan tin, crush it into a ball to soften, then open and lay inside the pastry so that it comes up the sides. Fill with baking beans or rice, then press down gently and bake for 10 minutes, or until firm. Remove the beans or rice and discard the paper. Return the pastry to the oven and continue to bake for 5–10 minutes, or until the pastry is dry. Remove and cool. Raise the oven temperature to moderately hot 190°C (375°F/Gas 5).
4 For the filling, heat the oil in a large saucepan. Add the onion and cook gently for 8 minutes, or until translucent. Raise the heat, add the sugar and cook for 5–10 minutes, or until the onion begins to caramelize. Next, pour in the wine and cook until the liquid has evaporated and the onion is soft. Season with salt and pepper. Remove from the pan and set aside.
5 In the pan, melt the butter, add the spinach and fry over high heat, stirring constantly, until the spinach is dry when pressed with the back of a spoon. (Wet spinach will make the quiche soggy.) Season with salt, pepper and the nutmeg, turn out on to a chopping board and chop finely.
6 In a saucepan, warm the cream and cheese gently, stirring, until the cheese melts, but does not boil. Season and cool before adding the egg. Fill the pastry case with the onion, then the spinach. Smooth the surface a little but do not pack down. Pour in the cream mixture and bake for 30 minutes, then lower the temperature to warm 160°C (315°F /Gas 2–3) and bake for 20 minutes to cook the centre of the quiche. Cover with foil if it is getting too brown. Serve warm.

Brie parcels with pears and almonds

A sophisticated brunch dish which may be served with grilled tomatoes, some watercress or a green salad. This would also make an elegant first course for a lunch or dinner party.

*Preparation time **25 minutes + 30 minutes chilling***
*Total cooking time **15 minutes***
Serves 4

120 g (4 oz) whole blanched almonds
1 large or 2 small ripe pears, peeled and thinly sliced
30 ml (1 fl oz) balsamic or tarragon vinegar
250 g (8 oz) ripe Brie
12 sheets filo pastry
150 g (5 oz) unsalted butter, melted

1 Preheat a grill to a high heat. Place the almonds into a food processor and blend for 30 seconds, or until they resemble fine breadcrumbs. Turn out onto a baking tray and place under the grill to toast. Do not walk away while this is happening as the almonds will burn very quickly. Season the toasted almonds with a little salt and pepper.

2 Place the pear slices in a bowl and sprinkle with the vinegar, toss to coat well and set aside. Cut the Brie in half through the middle to make two large flat pieces with a rind on one side of each. Lay one piece on a work surface, rind downwards, and place the pear slices on top of the cheese in a neat layer to completely cover the top of the cheese. You may need to do several layers in

order to use up all the pear. Sprinkle with any remaining vinegar, season with salt and pepper and place the second piece of Brie on top, so that the rind is uppermost and the edges are even all the way round. Wrap the cheese tightly in plastic wrap, place on a plate and chill for a minimum of 30 minutes. When chilled, cut into eight even-sized pieces and toss them in the almonds, taking care to keep the wedges whole.

3 Preheat the oven to hot 220°C (425°F/Gas 7). Brush one sheet of filo with the melted butter, cover with another sheet, brush again, then add a third sheet. Cut into two 20 cm (8 inch) squares. Discard the trimmings. Place one wedge of the Brie in the centre of each square and gather up the edges to form a purse, squeezing the pastry together to make a 'drawstring' effect. Brush gently with a little more butter. Repeat this process with the remaining pastry and Brie, making sure the Brie remains chilled or it will melt too quickly. When ready to cook, place the parcels on a greased baking tray and bake for 10 minutes, or until golden. Serve immediately.

Chef's tip A few ripe, peeled and sliced apricots or peeled seedless grapes can be used instead of the pears, or if time is limited, omit both the fruit and the vinegar and spread the opened-out cheese with 2 tablespoons of a fruit chutney instead.

Eastern rice pudding

The cardamom adds a distinctly Eastern flavour to this creamy rice pudding. Try serving it with the spicy fig conserve on page 51.

Preparation time **5 minutes**
Total cooking time **25 minutes**
Serves 4

seeds of 4 cardamom pods, crushed
400 ml (12³/4 fl oz) cream
400 ml (12³/4 fl oz) milk
75 g (2¹/2 oz) caster sugar
75 g (2¹/2 oz) short-grain rice

1 Combine the crushed cardamom pods, the cream and the milk in a medium saucepan. Bring to the boil, remove from the heat, cool slightly and stir in the sugar and rice. At this stage, the rice mixture can be refrigerated overnight or it can be cooked immediately.
2 Bring the rice mixture to the boil, lower the heat and cook, stirring constantly as it begins to thicken, for 20–25 minutes, or until the rice is just soft and the liquid has become creamy. The pudding should have a soft, flowing consistency and when a spoon is drawn through, the base of the pan should be seen and the pudding flow quickly to fill the parting behind it. (Remember that the rice will continue to thicken slightly when removed from the heat.) Serve with dried fruits or a fruit conserve.

Stewed rhubarb with ginger

This tangy rhubarb compote is enhanced by the colour and flavour of the redcurrant jelly and enlivened by the ginger.

Preparation time **10 minutes**
Total cooking time **20 minutes**
Serves 4

3 tablespoons redcurrant jelly
I kg (2 lb) rhubarb
30 g (I oz) crystallized or glacé ginger, finely chopped
a little caster or demerara sugar

1 In a small bowl, beat the redcurrant jelly with a spoon until smooth, pour into a wide pan and add 4 tablespoons water.
2 Trim and discard the leaves and the base of the stalks from the rhubarb. Cut the rhubarb into 2.5 cm (1 inch) slices and add to the pan in a single layer.
3 Bring to the boil and immediately turn the heat down to a bare simmer. Cover tightly with a lid or foil and cook for 10–15 minutes, or until tender. The rhubarb should still hold its shape. Be careful to cook very gently or you will end up with a purée.
4 Transfer to a bowl, add the ginger and taste. You may require a little caster or demerara sugar sprinkled over at this stage, depending on the acidity of the rhubarb. Leave to cool slightly and serve warm or, if you prefer, prepare the day before and chill overnight.

Chef's tip The acidity of the rhubarb will vary considerably so the recipe is only a guide as to sweetness. Add as much sugar as you require. Serve the rhubarb by itself or with thick yoghurt.

Eastern rice pudding (top left) and
Stewed rhubarb with ginger

Puff pastry with asparagus and mushrooms in creamy sauce

An ideal brunch dish: crisp in texture, the pastry is filled with subtle flavours that come together harmoniously in a creamy sauce.

Preparation time **30 minutes + 20 minutes chilling**
Total cooking time **25 minutes**
Makes 6

15 asparagus spears, trimmed
375 g (12 oz) ready-made block puff pastry
1 egg, beaten
45 g (1¹/2 oz) unsalted butter
30 g (1 oz) plain flour
250 ml (8 fl oz) milk
60 ml (2 fl oz) crème fraîche or cream
250 g (8 oz) button or oyster mushrooms,
    thickly sliced
melted butter, for brushing

1 Bring a pan of salted water to the boil. Add the asparagus spears and cook for 4 minutes, or until tender. Remove from the pan, plunge into a bowl of iced water, drain well and set aside.

2 On a lightly floured surface, roll the pastry to a rectangle approximately 20 x 30 cm (8 x 12 inches) and 5 mm (¹/4 inch) thick. With a large sharp knife, trim to straighten the two long sides and cut into two long strips. Now cut each strip into three diamonds or squares. Place them slightly apart on a damp baking tray and chill for 20 minutes.

3 Meanwhile, preheat the oven to moderately hot 200°C (400°F/Gas 6). Brush the top surface of the pastry with the beaten egg. Do not brush the edges of the pastry as the egg will set and prevent the pastry from rising. Lightly score the tops of the pastry cases in a crisscross pattern with a thin knife. Bake for about 10 minutes, or until well risen, crisp and golden. Split in two horizontally with a sharp knife. Scrape out and discard any soft dough.

4 In a medium saucepan, melt 30 g (1 oz) of the butter, add the flour and cook for 1 minute over low heat. Remove from the stove, pour in the milk and blend thoroughly with a wooden spoon or whisk. Return to low-medium heat, stir briskly until boiling and simmer for 2 minutes, stirring continuously. Add the crème fraîche or cream and stir over the heat for another minute. Remove from the stove and cover with foil. In a wide pan, melt the remaining butter and toss the mushrooms over medium heat for 2 minutes, or until cooked. Trim the asparagus tips to 6 cm (2¹/2 inch) lengths and reserve. Cut the remainder of the tender stalks into 2 cm (³/4 inch) lengths. Add the mushrooms and the small pieces of asparagus to the sauce and mix together briefly.

5 To assemble the pastry cases, spoon the warm sauce onto the six pastry bases and place the asparagus tips on top. Brush them with a little melted butter and replace the pastry lids. Warm through in the oven at warm 160°C (315°F/Gas 2–3) for 5 minutes before serving.

Chef's tips The pastry can be baked, split and scraped out the day before. Reheat in a warm oven before filling.

Note that you may have a little of the mushroom mixture left over after filling the pastry cases, depending on the size of asparagus you use. This is delicious eaten on toast as a snack.

Chocolate muffins

These rich dark chocolate muffins freeze very well—simply allow to cool completely and seal in airtight freezer containers or bags for up to 3 months. To serve, thaw at room temperature and reheat.

Preparation time **10 minutes**
Total cooking time **25 minutes**
Makes 12

210 g (6³/4 oz) plain flour
40 g (1¹/4 oz) cocoa powder
150 g (5 oz) caster sugar
2 teaspoons baking powder
250 ml (8 fl oz) milk
60 g (2 oz) unsalted butter, melted
¹/4 teaspoon vanilla extract or essence
120 g (4 oz) semi-sweet chocolate chips

1 Preheat the oven to moderate 180°C (350°F/Gas 4). Prepare a 12-hole (125 ml/4 fl oz capacity) muffin tin by buttering well or lining with paper cups.
2 Sift together the flour, cocoa powder, sugar, baking powder and a pinch of salt into a bowl.
3 In a small bowl, mix together the milk, melted butter and vanilla.
4 Make a well in the centre of the dry ingredients and pour in the milk mixture. Stir until the liquid is just barely mixed in. The batter is supposed to be lumpy so do not overmix.
5 Gently fold in the chocolate chips. Place the mixture in the prepared muffin tin, filling each cup three-quarters full. Bake for 20–25 minutes, or until a toothpick inserted into the centre of a muffin comes out clean. Unmould and cool on a wire rack. Serve warm or cold.

Bacon and cheese cornbreads

These individual American cornbreads are quick to prepare and taste delicious served warm. As an alternative, try serving with a bowl of hearty soup for lunch on a cold winter's day.

Preparation time **20 minutes**
Total cooking time **20 minutes**
Makes 12

140 g (4¹/2 oz) yellow cornmeal
140 g (4¹/2 oz) plain flour
30 g (1 oz) caster sugar
1 teaspoon baking powder
1 teaspoon salt
290 ml (9¹/2 fl oz) buttermilk
2 eggs
70 g (2¹/4 oz) unsalted butter, melted
120 g (4 oz) Cheddar cheese, cut
   into small cubes
90 g (3 oz) bacon, cooked and diced

1 Preheat the oven to moderate 180°C (350°F/Gas 4). Prepare a 12-hole (125 ml/4 fl oz capacity) muffin tin by buttering well or lining with paper cups.
2 Sift together the cornmeal, flour, sugar, baking powder and salt into a bowl.
3 In a separate bowl, whisk together the buttermilk, eggs and melted butter. Make a well in the centre of the dry ingredients and pour in the buttermilk mixture. Mix until just barely combined. Add the diced cheese and bacon and fold in. The batter should be thick and lumpy—do not overmix.
4 Place the mixture in the prepared tin, filling the cups three-quarters full. Bake for 15–20 minutes, or until lightly coloured and a toothpick inserted into the centre of a muffin comes out clean. Unmould immediately and cool on a wire rack.

Chocolate muffins (top) and Bacon and cheese cornbreads

Eggs Florentine

A classic dish made from a layer of spinach and lightly poached eggs topped with a creamy cheese sauce. For perfect poached eggs, use the freshest eggs possible.

Preparation time **25 minutes**
Total cooking time **30 minutes**
Serves 4

MORNAY SAUCE
15 g (¹/₂ oz) unsalted butter
2 tablespoons plain flour
250 ml (8 fl oz) milk
pinch of ground nutmeg
40 g (1¹/₄ oz) Gruyère cheese, grated
2 egg yolks

60 g (2 oz) unsalted butter
500 g (1 lb) English spinach leaves, cleaned
3 tablespoons vinegar
8 very fresh eggs

1 To make the mornay sauce, melt the butter in a heavy-based pan over low-medium heat. Sprinkle the flour over the butter and cook for 1–2 minutes without allowing it to colour, stirring constantly with a wooden spoon. Remove the pan from the heat and slowly add the milk, whisking or beating vigorously to avoid lumps.

Return to medium heat and bring to the boil, stirring constantly. Simmer for 3–4 minutes, or until the sauce coats the back of a spoon. Stir in the nutmeg, then remove from the heat. Set aside, covered, and keep warm.
2 In a large shallow pan, melt the butter over low heat and add the spinach. Cook for about 5–8 minutes, or until dry. Set aside and keep warm.
3 Whisk the cheese into the mornay sauce, then whisk in the egg yolks. Season, to taste, with salt and pepper. Place over low heat and mix until the cheese is melted, then heat until very hot but not boiling. Set aside, cover the surface with a piece of baking paper and keep warm.
4 Place 2 litres water in a large pan and bring to the boil over high heat. Reduce the temperature to low and add the vinegar. The water should be barely simmering.
5 Crack the eggs one at a time into a cup or bowl and carefully slide into the vinegared water two or three at a time. Cook for 2–3 minutes, or until the egg white is firm but not hard. Very gently remove, using a slotted spoon and drain thoroughly.
6 Divide the cooked spinach evenly among four warmed plates. Place two poached eggs in the centre of the spinach and cover with the hot mornay sauce. Serve immediately.

Spinach and crab roulade

*Thick slices of light spinach roulade with a creamy crab filling are perfect for brunch,
a light lunch or served as a first course.*

Preparation time **45 minutes**
Total cooking time **40 minutes**
Serves 6

FILLING
20 g (³/4 oz) unsalted butter
I tablespoon plain flour
200 ml (6¹/2 fl oz) milk
**225 g (7¹/4 oz) white crab meat, fresh,
    frozen or tinned**
pinch of cayenne pepper

ROULADE
**450 g (14¹/4 oz) English spinach, large stalks removed,
    or 185 g (6 oz) frozen spinach**
15 g (¹/2 oz) unsalted butter, melted
4 eggs, separated
pinch of ground nutmeg

1 To make the filling, melt the butter in a heavy-based pan over low-medium heat. Sprinkle the flour over the butter and cook for 1 minute without allowing it to colour, stirring constantly with a wooden spoon. Remove the pan from the heat and slowly add the milk, whisking or beating vigorously to avoid lumps. Return to low heat and briskly stir with a wooden spoon or whisk until the mixture is smooth and begins to thicken, then turn up the heat and stir briskly until boiling. Simmer for 3–4 minutes, or until the sauce coats the back of a spoon. Cover with a piece of buttered greaseproof paper pressed onto the surface and set aside.

2 To make the roulade, line a swiss roll or baking tin, approximately 30 x 25 cm (12 x 10 inches) with non-stick baking paper. If using fresh spinach, half fill a large pan with water and bring to the boil, add a generous pinch of salt and the spinach. Return to the boil and cook for 1–2 minutes, then drain in a colander or sieve, run under cold water and squeeze out the excess water. Chop finely, using a large sharp knife. If using frozen spinach, thaw, drain, squeeze out the excess water and chop finely. Put the fresh or frozen spinach in a large bowl and add the butter.

3 Preheat the oven to moderately hot 200°C (400°F/ Gas 6). Stir the egg yolks and nutmeg into the spinach and season well. In a large bowl, whisk the egg whites until stiff and standing in peaks, then stir a large tablespoon of egg white into the spinach mixture to loosen it. Add the remaining egg white in one addition, then using a large metal spoon, carefully cut and fold into the spinach. Pour into the prepared tin, lightly smoothing it to the edges with a palette knife. Bake for about 10 minutes, or until the mixture is just set and springs back to the light touch of a finger. Meanwhile, spread a tea towel onto the work surface and cover it with non-stick baking paper.

4 Reheat the filling mixture, then stir in the crab, cayenne pepper and salt and pepper, to taste, and heat right through.

5 Turn the spinach roulade over onto the paper and tea towel and remove the tin and the paper lining. Quickly spread with the crab filling, then with the shortest edge towards you, pick up the cloth and the paper and push the roulade away from you, holding it quite low, so that the roulade rolls up like a swiss roll. Stop when the last of the roulade is underneath, then lift it onto a dish. Cut into thick slices and serve immediately.

Chef's tip This is perfect to serve alone, but can also be served with a sauce such as hollandaise or Béarnaise.

Twice-baked individual cheese soufflés

A soufflé with a difference—you can relax! Prepare these individual soufflés the day before and watch them rise again ready to thrill your brunch guests.

*Preparation time **35 minutes + cooling time***
*Total cooking time **45 minutes***
*Serves **8***

315 ml (10 fl oz) milk
tiny pinch of grated nutmeg
1 small bay leaf
1 small French shallot, halved
4 whole peppercorns
30 g (1 oz) unsalted butter
**30 g (1 oz) potato flour or 15 g (¹/2 oz) flour mixed
   with 15 g (¹/2 oz) cornflour**
15 g (¹/2 oz) unsalted butter, cut into very small cubes
3 eggs, separated
90 g (3 oz) Cheddar
¹/4 teaspoon dry mustard powder
1 egg white
155 ml (5 fl oz) cream
2 tablespoons grated Parmesan or Gruyère cheese

1 In a small saucepan, warm the milk with the nutmeg, bay leaf, shallot and peppercorns. When bubbles form around the edge of the pan, remove from the stove.

2 Melt the butter in a large saucepan, remove from the heat and stir in the potato flour. Strain the milk and pour into the pan, blend well and return to the heat. Whisk briskly until the mixture comes to the boil. Remove from the stove and scatter the butter cubes over the surface. Cover the pan with a lid and leave to cool slightly. Meanwhile, preheat the oven to moderate 180°C (350°F/Gas 4). Lightly butter eight small soufflé dishes or ramekins of 150 ml (5 fl oz) capacity.

3 Uncover the sauce and stir in the melted layer of butter, followed by the egg yolks, Cheddar, mustard, and salt and pepper, to taste. In a large bowl, whisk the four egg whites until stiff. Using a large metal spoon or a spatula, stir 1 tablespoon of the egg white into the cheese mixture to loosen it, then add the remainder in one go, carefully folding until just combined.

4 Divide the mixture among the soufflé dishes, pouring it in gently to avoid losing any volume. Place the dishes in a roasting tin or deep ovenproof dish and pour in enough warm water to come three quarters of the way up the sides of the dishes. Bake for 25 minutes, or until the soufflés have lightly risen and are firm to the touch. Remove from the water and leave to cool. (Cover and keep overnight in the refrigerator if you wish to prepare the night before.)

5 Just before serving, preheat the oven to moderately hot 200°C (400°F/Gas 6). Return the soufflé dishes to their ovenproof dish, pour some cream into each, dividing it equally, and season each one lightly. Sprinkle with Parmesan and pour warm water around to come three quarters of the way up the sides of the dishes, as before. Bake for 10–15 minutes, or until risen and golden brown. Lift out carefully and place each dish on to a plate. Serve immediately.

Devilled kidneys with sage polenta discs

These herb and polenta discs are a modern alternative to the more usual toast when serving devilled kidneys for breakfast or brunch.

Preparation time **40 minutes + 1 hour resting**
Total cooking time **25 minutes**
Serves 4–6

SAGE POLENTA DISCS
600 ml (20 fl oz) milk
25 g (3/4 oz) unsalted butter
175 g (5³/4 oz) precooked cornmeal or instant polenta
50 g (1³/4 oz) Parmesan, freshly grated
30 g (1 oz) fresh sage, finely chopped

oil, for deep-frying

DEVILLED KIDNEYS
8 lambs kidneys
1¹/2 tablespoons tomato chutney
¹/2 teaspoon mustard
dash of Worcestershire sauce
small pinch of cayenne pepper
60 g (2 oz) unsalted butter
1 French shallot, chopped
2–3 tablespoons beef or vegetable stock

1 To prepare the sage polenta discs, heat the milk and butter in a large pan until nearly boiling. Using a whisk, briskly beat in the cornmeal and stir continuously over medium heat for 2–3 minutes, or until thick. Remove and cool for 1 minute. Add the Parmesan and sage, season well with salt and pepper, and cool for another 5 minutes. Lightly flour the work surface and roll or press out the polenta to a thickness of 1 cm (1/2 inch). Leave to cool and firm for 1 hour. Using a 5 cm (2 inch) plain cutter, cut out 25–30 discs. Place the discs in a single layer on two trays lined with baking paper and cover until needed.

2 To prepare the devilled kidneys, remove the fat and fine membrane from around the kidneys, then lay them flat, hold in place with one hand and cut each through sideways with a sharp knife. Using the tip of a sharp knife or scissors, trim away the core from the cut side of each kidney half. In a small bowl, stir together the tomato chutney, mustard, Worcestershire sauce and cayenne pepper. In a wide frying pan, melt half the butter and, over a medium heat, cook the shallot for 3–4 minutes, or until golden. Transfer the shallot to a plate, wipe out the pan with paper towels and set aside.

3 Heat the oven to very slow 120°C (250°F/Gas 1/2). Fill a deep-fryer or large pan one third full of oil and heat to 180°C (350°F) (a cube of bread dropped into the oil will brown in 15 seconds). Deep-fry the sage polenta discs in small batches for 2–3 minutes, remove from the oil and drain on crumpled paper towels. Transfer to a wire rack and keep the discs warm in the oven, uncovered to retain their crispness.

4 Melt the remaining butter in the frying pan. When sizzling hot, add the kidneys, skin-side-down first. Cook over high heat for 20 seconds, turn over and cook for another 20 seconds. Remove to the plate with the shallot. Lower the heat, add the mustard mixture from the bowl to the pan and stir for a moment to blend. Return the kidneys and the shallot to the pan and toss for 1–2 minutes, or until cooked through. Put four or five polenta discs on each plate and divide the kidneys among them. Add the stock to the pan and cook for 1 minute, stirring to blend in the kidney juices. Pour the sauce over the kidneys and serve immediately.

Chef's tip The devilled kidneys could be served just on toast. The sage and polenta discs would be an excellent accompaniment to serve with fried or scrambled eggs, grilled tomatoes or sausages.

Home-made sausage patties

These quick and easy minced pork patties can be served simply with grilled tomatoes or as part of a full traditional cooked breakfast.

Preparation time **5 minutes**
Total cooking time **4–6 minutes**
Makes **8**

I teaspoon salt
¹/4 teaspoon ground black pepper
pinch of fennel seeds
¹/4 teaspoon paprika
400 g (12³/4 oz) pork mince
I tablespoon oil

1 In a bowl, mix the salt, pepper, fennel and paprika with the pork mince. Mix in 2 tablespoons cold water. To check the seasoning, fry a little of the mixture until it is cooked through and taste it. Divide the seasoned meat into eight balls. Flatten each ball to make a patty about 1 cm (¹/2 inch) thick.
2 Heat the oil in a frying pan over medium heat. Cook the sausage patties in batches for 3–5 minutes on each side, or until browned and cooked through. Keep warm until ready to serve.

Potato griddle scones

These scones are delicious served with grilled bacon—or simply butter, jam or honey—as a leisurely brunch or breakfast.

Preparation time **10 minutes**
Total cooking time **45 minutes**
Makes **12 scones**

500 g (I lb) potatoes
60 g (2 oz) unsalted butter, at room temperature
60 g (2 oz) plain flour
I teaspoon baking powder
large pinch of grated nutmeg

1 Peel the potatoes and put them in a large pan of salted water. Bring to the boil, then reduce the heat and simmer until tender, approximately 30–35 minutes. Drain well, then return to the pan to dry over low heat.
2 Mash the potato until smooth, then beat in the butter. Sift the flour, baking powder, nutmeg and some salt into a bowl. Add the mashed potato and, using a round-bladed knife, bring the mixture together. You will need to use the mixture at once as baking powder is activated by moisture and warmth.
3 On a lightly floured surface, pat out the mixture to a 1.5 cm (⁵/8 inch) thickness. Using a 4 cm (1¹/2 inch) plain cutter, cut out 12 rounds. Heat a heavy-based frying pan or griddle over medium heat and dust lightly with flour. Cook the scones for about 8 minutes, or until cooked through, turning after 4 minutes. Serve warm.

Home-made sausage patties (top) and Potato griddle scones

Croissants

Croissants require time and effort to produce, but the rich buttery result will astound friends and family. Served warm with jam or marmalade, they are guaranteed to disappear at an alarming rate! On page 62 there are step-by-step illustrations showing how to make croissants.

Preparation time **3 hours + resting + chilling overnight**
Total cooking time **20 minutes**
Makes 12–16

500 g (1 lb) plain flour
1 teaspoon salt
50 g (1³/4 oz) caster sugar
320 ml (10 fl oz) milk
15 g (¹/2 oz) fresh yeast or 7 g (¹/4 oz) dried yeast
340 g (10³/4 oz) unsalted butter, at room temperature
1 egg, beaten

1 Sift the flour, salt and sugar into a large bowl and make a well in the centre. Heat the milk to warm, stir in the yeast and 1 tablespoon of the flour until dissolved, then leave to stand until bubbles form. Add to the dry ingredients and bring together to form a soft dough, then tip out onto a floured work surface and knead for 5 minutes, or until smooth and elastic. Transfer the dough to a floured bowl and cover. Set aside in a warm area for about 1 hour, or until doubled in volume.

2 Meanwhile, put the butter between two sheets of plastic wrap and roll into a rectangle measuring about 20 x 10 cm (8 x 4 inches). Refrigerate until ready to use.

3 Once the dough has risen, punch it down and transfer to a floured work surface. Roll into a rectangle about 40 x 12 cm (16 x 5 inches). The dough should be just over twice as long as the butter and a little bit wider. Place the butter on the lower half of the dough and fold the dough over to completely enclose the butter. Seal the edges with your fingertips. Turn the dough so that the fold is on the right-hand side and lightly roll the dough into a large rectangle twice as long as it is wide. Brush off excess flour and fold the dough into even thirds like a letter, with the bottom third up and the top third down. Chill in plastic wrap for 20 minutes.

4 Remove from the refrigerator and, with the fold on the right-hand side, roll out the dough as above. Fold it as before and chill. Repeat again.

5 Remove the dough from the refrigerator and cut it in half. On a well-floured surface, roll each piece of the dough into a large rectangle, and trim it to 22 x 36 cm (8³/4 x 14¹/2 inches). Using a triangular template with a base of 18 cm (7 inches) and sides of 14 cm (5¹/2 inches), cut the rectangle into six triangles (you should also be left with two end triangles). Roll the dough up, starting from the wide end, to form crescents. Place the croissants on baking trays and lightly brush with the beaten egg. Cover with plastic wrap and refrigerate overnight.

6 Remove the croissants from the refrigerator and set aside to rise for about 30–45 minutes, or until double in size. Do not try to hurry the process by putting them anywhere too warm, or the butter in the dough will melt. Preheat the oven to moderately hot 200°C (400°F/Gas 6).

7 Once the croissants have doubled in size, gently brush with a second layer of the beaten egg. Bake for about 15–20 minutes, or until golden brown.

Chef's tip It is very important that the dough and the butter are at the same consistency before rolling in. If the butter is too soft, it will seep out as the dough is rolled, and if it is too hard, it will crack and break, leaving the final product with uneven layers. The butter should feel a little firmer than cream cheese.

Crumpets

Light and airy crumpets toasted on a fork in front of an open fire have always been a tea-time delight, but they also make a special treat for breakfast and may be toasted under the grill or in a toaster.

Preparation time **10 minutes + 1 hour 50 minutes standing**
Total cooking time **45 minutes**
Makes 8 crumpets

375 ml (12 fl oz) milk
15 g (¹/2 oz) fresh yeast or 7 g (¹/4 oz) dried yeast
375 g (12 oz) plain flour
¹/2 teaspoon salt
¹/2 teaspoon bicarbonate of soda
oil or clarified butter, for cooking

1 Pour the milk into a saucepan and heat until warm, remove from the heat and stir in the yeast.

2 Sift the flour and the salt into a bowl and make a well in the centre. Pour in a little of the milk mixture and beat with a whisk, electric beaters or your hand to bring in a little of the flour, mixing to a smooth paste. Repeat this process until all the liquid has been added and all the flour drawn in, then beat until completely smooth. Cover with a plate or plastic wrap and leave in a warm place for approximately 1–1¹/2 hours, or until doubled in size and full of bubbles. Dissolve the bicarbonate of soda in 200 ml (6¹/2 fl oz) water. Add it to the batter and mix well. Cover and set aside for 15–20 minutes.

3 On the top of the stove, heat a griddle pan or a wide heavy-based frying pan to medium heat and brush with a little oil or clarified butter. Lightly butter or oil the inside of two or more 9–10 cm (3¹/2–4 inch) pastry cutters or crumpet rings, and put them on the pan.

4 Pour in the crumpet batter to a thickness of 1 cm (¹/2 inch), lower the heat to very low and cook for 7–8 minutes. The bubbles will rise as the crumpets cook. The crumpets are ready to turn over when the top has dried out enough to form a skin (see Chef's techniques, page 63). Loosen the rings, turn the crumpets over and brown the second side for 1–2 minutes. Remove and cool on a wire rack, covered with a tea towel to prevent drying out. Repeat with the remaining batter as the rings become free. If the batter thickens on standing, add a little more water to thin it.

5 To serve, preheat a grill to the highest setting and toast the crumpets well on the first cooked side, then brown more lightly on the second side. Spread the lightly grilled side with butter and serve straight away.

Chef's tip If you have any fresh yeast left over, it can be stored in the refrigerator, lightly wrapped in greaseproof paper, for up to 2 weeks.

Fig conserve

With fabulous soft, spicy flavours of the Orient, this conserve makes a memorable accompaniment to Eastern rice pudding, or indeed any of the sweet pancake recipes. Try a spoonful with a bowl of porridge.

Preparation time **10 minutes**
Total cooking time **1 hour 5 minutes**
Makes approximately 1 litre

1 lemon
1 lime
2 whole star anise
2 cloves
900 g (1 lb 13 oz) fresh black, purple or green figs, stalks removed and cut into quarters
75 ml (2¹/2 fl oz) red wine
450 g (14¹/4 oz) caster sugar

1 Roughly chop the lemon and lime and place into a square of muslin with the star anise and cloves. Tie into a purse, securing with string and leaving the ends long.
2 Combine the figs and red wine with 75 ml (2¹/2 fl oz) water in a large pan with a lid and tie the string of the muslin bag to the pan handle, so that the bag will be suspended in the figs. Simmer gently for 15 minutes.
3 Squeeze the muslin bag against the side of the pan with a spoon and then remove and discard. (Be careful as it will be very hot.) Stir the sugar into the mixture in the pan over low heat until the sugar dissolves.
4 Raise the heat and boil, bubbling hard, until thick and syrupy. Start checking the consistency (see Chef's techniques, page 63) from 20 minutes onwards. Continue boiling and testing for setting every 5 minutes. Remember that the conserve will thicken a little more as it cools. Refrigerate and use within 2 weeks.

Chef's tip Conserves do not have the long storage life of jams as there is not enough sugar to preserve the fruit.

Kumquat conserve

Bettering a good home-made marmalade for breakfast is difficult, but this bright and zesty preserve is sure to become a favourite. Kumquats, originally native to China, are small bittersweet fruits with edible skins.

Preparation time **10 minutes + overnight standing**
Total cooking time **40 minutes**
Makes approximately 1 litre

675 g (1 lb 6 oz) ripe kumquats
675 g (1 lb 6 oz) caster sugar
80 ml (2³/4 oz) gin

1 Roughly chop the kumquats into fairly small pieces and layer in a large bowl with the sugar. Cover and leave to stand overnight. You may, depending on the ripeness of the fruit, be able to reduce this time by an hour or so; however, the sugar should be virtually dissolved and the juice running out of the kumquats.
2 Tip the fruits and all the sugary juices into a large pan and add 300 ml (9¹/2 fl oz) water. Slowly heat until any remaining sugar dissolves, stirring to prevent any of it catching on the bottom of the pan.
3 Raise the heat and boil hard for 15–20 minutes, or until thick, but not too syrupy. Do not stir. Remove the pan from the heat, stir in the gin and test for setting (see Chef's techniques, page 63). If not set, continue boiling and testing for setting every 5 minutes. Refrigerate and use within 2 weeks.

Chef's tip Kumquat pips, unlike orange pips, are perfectly edible when cooked, and add a delicate nuttiness to this conserve, quite apart from being attractive. You could, of course, pick out all the pips as you cut up the kumquats. You should then place all the pips into a muslin bag and add it to the pan with the water, removing it when the conserve has reached setting point.

Fig conserve (top) and Kumquat conserve

Pikelets

These small thick pancakes are known as Scotch pancakes in England and are served hot and buttered with a fruity or a sweet accompaniment.

*Preparation time **8 minutes + 1 hour refrigeration***
*Total cooking time **15 minutes***
*Makes **12***

I egg, beaten
50 g (1³/4 oz) caster sugar
25 g (³/4 oz) unsalted butter
280 ml (9 fl oz) milk
225 g (7¹/4 oz) plain flour
¹/2 teaspoon bicarbonate of soda
¹/2 teaspoon baking powder
¹/2 teaspoon cream of tartar

1 In a small bowl, beat the egg with half the sugar. In a small pan, melt the butter with the rest of the sugar. Remove from the heat and add the milk and 1 teaspoon cold water to the pan.

2 Sift together the flour, bicarbonate of soda, baking powder, cream of tartar and a pinch of salt into a large bowl. Make a well in the centre. Pour the egg mixture and butter mixture into the well and beat with a wooden spoon or balloon whisk until the dry ingredients have disappeared and a smooth batter is formed. Cover and refrigerate for 1 hour or overnight.

3 Brush a large non-stick frying pan or griddle with melted butter and place over high heat. Using 2 tablespoons of mixture for each, drop the pikelets into the pan and cook for 1 minute, or until bubbles rise to the surface. Turn them over and cook for 1 minute, or until lightly golden. Serve immediately, or keep warm, wrapped in foil, in a low oven.

Chef's tip Serve with butter, lemon juice and sugar, maple syrup or fresh fruit conserves.

Waffles

Waffles, made from a light sweetened batter, have a honeycombed surface ideal for holding large quantities of sweet runny syrup or honey for those with a particularly sweet tooth.

*Preparation time **5 minutes***
*Total cooking time **5 minutes per waffle***
*Makes **about 8–10 waffles***

250 g (8 oz) plain flour
I tablespoon caster sugar
1¹/2 teaspoons baking powder
¹/2 teaspoon salt
375 ml (12 fl oz) milk or buttermilk
30 g (1 oz) unsalted butter, melted
2 eggs

1 Sift together the flour, sugar, baking powder and salt into a large bowl.

2 In a separate bowl, combine the milk, melted butter and eggs. Gradually add to the flour mixture and mix until well combined.

3 Preheat a waffle iron according to the manufacturer's instructions. Once hot, lightly brush with oil. Pour in the recommended amount of batter and cook until golden brown in colour and crispy. Serve with whipped butter and honey or maple syrup.

Brioche

Brioche, a light yeast dough enriched with butter and eggs, is wonderful served with butter and jam for breakfast or tea, or alternatively as an accompaniment to stewed fruit. There are many different ways to mould brioche dough—in this recipe it has been moulded into the traditional 'brioche à tête', where the small ball on the top represents the 'head' of the brioche. See page 62 for step-by-step instructions.

Preparation time **30 minutes + 4 hours rising**
Total cooking time **25 minutes**
Makes 1 large loaf or 4 small loaves

2 tablespoons warm milk
15 g (¹/₂ oz) fresh yeast or 7 g (¹/₄ oz) dried yeast
375 g (12 oz) strong or plain flour
55 g (1³/₄ oz) caster sugar
1 teaspoon salt
6 eggs, lightly beaten
175 g (5³/₄ oz) unsalted butter, at room temperature
1 egg, beaten and mixed with 2 tablespoons of water, for glazing

1 Pour the milk into a bowl and dissolve the yeast in it. Add 1 tablespoon of the flour, cover and set aside until bubbles start to appear. Sift the remaining flour, sugar and salt into a large bowl, make a well in the centre and add the beaten eggs and yeast mixture. Draw the flour into the wet ingredients to make a sticky dough, then transfer to a floured surface.
2 Lift and throw the dough down on the work surface with floured hands for 20 minutes, or until the dough forms a smooth ball. Place in an oiled bowl and turn the

dough over to coat with the oil. Cover and let rise at room temperature for 2–2¹/₂ hours, or until doubled in volume.
3 Turn out the dough, punch down, cover and leave to rest for 5 minutes, then transfer to the work surface again. Place the soft butter on top of the dough and pinch and squeeze the two of them together until they are well combined. Knead for 5 more minutes, or until the dough is smooth again. Cover and let rest for 5 minutes.
4 Brush a 1.2 litre capacity brioche mould or four small 425 ml (15 fl oz) capacity brioche moulds liberally with melted butter. If using the small moulds, divide the dough in four. Set aside a quarter of each piece of dough. Form the large pieces into balls and drop them into the moulds seam-side-down. Make a hole in the top of each ball using your finger and form the reserved pieces into tear-drop shapes to fit into the holes. Press down to seal. Cover and leave to rise for 1–1¹/₂ hours, or until the moulds are half to three-quarters full. Preheat the oven to moderately hot 200°C (400°F/Gas 6). Lightly brush with the egg glaze and bake for 20–25 minutes, or until a nice golden brown. Turn out and allow to cool on a wire rack.

Chef's tip For raisin brioche, soak 2 tablespoons raisins in some rum to plump them up. Drain and add to the dough after the butter has been incorporated.

Sour cherry pecan bread

If dried sour cherries or muscatels are difficult to obtain, roughly chopped dried apricots may be substituted, just as hazelnuts may be used in place of the pecans.

*Preparation time **10 minutes***
*Total cooking time **1 hour 5 minutes***
Serves 6–8

120 g (4 oz) caster sugar
175 g (5¾ oz) golden syrup
250 ml (8 fl oz) milk
1 egg, beaten
250 g (8 oz) plain flour
1 teaspoon ground cinnamon
3 teaspoons baking powder
60 g (2 oz) dried sour cherries, chopped, or
    muscatel raisins
60 g (2 oz) pecan nuts, roughly chopped

1 Brush a loaf tin 22 x 12.5 x 6 cm (9 x 5 x 2½ inches) with melted butter and line with baking paper, letting it hang over the two longest sides. Preheat the oven to moderate 180°C (350°F/Gas 4).

2 In a pan over low heat, warm the sugar, syrup and milk and stir until the sugar dissolves. Remove from the heat and set aside to cool to lukewarm. Stir in the egg.

3 Sift the flour, cinnamon, baking powder and a pinch of salt into a bowl and toss in the sour cherries or raisins and pecans. Add the syrup mixture and stir quickly until all the ingredients are combined. Pour immediately into the loaf tin and bake for 1 hour. (Cover loosely with foil after 30 minutes if the bread appears to be browning too quickly.) The bread will be done when the surface springs back when lightly pressed with your fingertips.

4 Leave to cool for 10 minutes, then turn out onto a wire rack. The bread improves with keeping and can be stored, wrapped in plastic wrap or foil, for up to 2 weeks in a cool place. Serve plain or buttered.

Danish pastries

Although this recipe may be time-consuming, nothing quite matches the taste of this freshly made, rich and flaky yeast dough.

Preparation time **3 hours + refrigeration**
Total cooking time **30 minutes**
Makes **28**

1 kg (2 lb) strong or plain flour
90 g (3 oz) caster sugar
20 g (³/4 oz) salt
30 g (1 oz) fresh yeast or 15 g (¹/2 oz) dried yeast
700 ml (23¹/4 fl oz) warm milk
450 g (14¹/4 oz) unsalted butter, chilled
1 egg, beaten
50 g (1³/4 oz) flaked almonds
icing sugar, to dust

PASSION FRUIT CREAM FILLING
30 g (1 oz) caster sugar
2 large egg yolks
2 teaspoons plain flour
2 teaspoons cornflour
125 ml (4 fl oz) passion fruit juice or pulp

OR

ORANGE CREAM FILLING
30 g (1 oz) caster sugar
2 large egg yolks
2 teaspoons plain flour
2 teaspoons cornflour
125 ml (4 fl oz) orange juice

1 Butter and flour a baking tray. Sift the flour, sugar and salt into a large bowl and make a well in the centre. Cream the yeast with 50 ml (1³/4 fl oz) of the milk. Stir in the remaining milk and pour into the well in the dry ingredients. Draw in the flour with your fingers until the mixture forms a soft dough. Knead the dough on a floured surface until it is smooth and elastic. Cover with plastic wrap in a bowl and chill for 10 minutes.

2 To make the passion fruit cream filling, place the sugar, egg yolks, flour and cornflour in a medium bowl and mix well. Bring the juice to the boil in a medium saucepan. Add a little to the sugar mixture, stir to blend, then add the sugar mixture to the saucepan. Bring the mixture to the boil, stirring continuously, and cook for 1 minute. Cover and leave to cool.

3 To make the orange cream filling, proceed exactly as for the passion fruit filling above, using the orange juice instead of the passion fruit juice.

4 On a floured surface, roll out the dough into a rectangle three times as long as it is wide, and 3 mm (¹/8 inch) thick. Tap and roll out the butter within two long sheets of plastic wrap into a rectangle, the same width as, but two thirds the length of, the dough. Unwrap and lay the butter on the top two thirds of the dough. Fold the exposed third of the dough up over the butter and fold the top third down.

5 Turn the dough to look like a book, with the binding on the left, and roll again into a rectangle and fold into three. Repeat twice, wrapping in plastic wrap and chilling for 20 minutes between each roll.

6 On a floured surface, roll the dough into a square or rectangle 3 mm (¹/8 inch) thick. Cut into rectangles 10 x 13 cm (4 x 5 inches) and place on the baking tray.

7 To make the Danish pastries, preheat the oven to moderately hot 200°C (400°F/Gas 6). Spoon the filling into a piping bag and pipe into the centre of each pastry. Draw up the corners and press together firmly. Set aside in a warm place to prove for 30 minutes. Brush with the egg, avoiding the sides of the pastry as this will prevent the dough from rising as it cooks. Sprinkle with a few flaked almonds and bake for 15–20 minutes, or until golden. Cool on wire racks and dust with sifted icing sugar, if desired.

Red fruit conserve

This dark red fruit conserve may be used in the same way as jam although it has a shorter storage life.
It is simply delicious served with buttered toast, brioche, waffles or used as a filling in pancakes.

Preparation time **5 minutes**
Total cooking time **1 hour 30 minutes**
Makes about 750 ml (24 fl oz)

1 kg (2 lb) mixed fresh or frozen soft red fruits
1 kg (2 lb) sugar

1 Combine the fruit and sugar with 3 tablespoons water in a large pan and slowly heat for 3–4 minutes, or until the sugar has dissolved, stirring to prevent the sugar from catching on the bottom of the pan. Put two or three saucers or small plates in the freezer.
2 Raise the heat and boil rapidly until syrupy and jam-like in consistency. Skim off any scum that forms on the surface. The cooking may take from 30 minutes to 1 1/2 hours, depending on the acidity in your choice of fruits. Start checking for consistency after 30 minutes, by drawing a spoon through the mixture to see if it 'parts'. If it does, pick up a little conserve on the spoon and tip it to the side. If it falls in heavy drops from the spoon, it is ready for the final test. To do the final test on the conserve, put a teaspoon of conserve on one of the cold saucers, allow the conserve to cool slightly and press lightly forward with your index finger. If the setting point is reached, the conserve should have a slight skin, which will wrinkle as you press. Also, if you draw your finger through the conserve, the conserve will stay separated and not run back together (see Chef's techniques, page 63). If the mixture is not ready, reboil it, testing it every 5 minutes until it is. Do not overboil or the fruit will lose its colour and have a caramelized flavour.
3 When ready, remove from the heat and cool. Stir again to disperse the fruit and then spoon into clean bowls or sterilised jars.

Chef's tip This conserve may be served immediately or covered and refrigerated for up to 2 weeks. Conserves do not have the long storage life of jams as there is not enough sugar in them to preserve the fruit for as long.

Chef's techniques

♦

Croissants

Folding the butter into the dough and refolding creates layers that puff up when cooked.

When the dough has risen, punch it down, then roll it out to a rectangle just over twice as long as the butter and a little wider. Put the butter on the lower half of the dough and bring the dough over to enclose it.

Turn the dough so the fold is on the right, then roll out into a rectangle. Fold the dough into even thirds, like a letter, with the bottom third up and the top third down. Chill, then repeat twice.

Cut the dough in half and roll out into two large rectangles. Using a triangular template, cut the rectangles into six triangles (you will be left with the two end pieces).

Roll the triangles from the wide end, to form crescents.

Brioche

Brioche dough is not as firm as bread dough and the butter needs to be beaten in.

Lightly flour your hands and lift and throw the dough down on a work surface for about 20 minutes, or until the dough forms a smooth ball.

After the dough has risen, punch it down, cover and leave it for 5 minutes. Transfer it to the work surface and blend in the butter, pinching and squeezing the two of them together until well combined.

Knead for 5 minutes, or until the dough is quite smooth.

Form the large pieces of dough into balls and drop them into the moulds seam-side-down. Make a hole in the top with your finger and fit the small tear-drop pieces of dough into the holes. Press down to seal.

Bagels

The secret to making bagels is the process of boiling before baking, creating the chewy texture.

Roll the dough into tight balls, poke your finger through the centre and gently enlarge the hole until the dough resembles a doughnut.

Cook the bagels in simmering water for 1 minute each side.

Brush the bagels with beaten egg before baking for 20–25 minutes. They can be sprinkled with poppy or sesame seeds before baking.

Hollandaise sauce

This sauce must not be allowed to get too hot, otherwise it may curdle.

Whisk the egg yolks and water together in a heatproof bowl until foamy. Place the bowl over a pan half-filled with simmering water and whisk until thick. The bowl should not touch the water. Gradually whisk in the butter.

Continue adding the melted butter, over very low heat, whisking constantly. The sauce should leave a trail on the surface when the whisk is lifted.

Once all the butter is incorporated, strain the sauce into a clean bowl, stir in the lemon juice and then season with salt and pepper.

Crumpets

Crumpets are delicious when freshly made at home and are not difficult to make.

Cook the crumpets until bubbles appear. They are ready to turn over when the top has dried out enough to form a skin.

Testing fruit conserve

When testing for setting, use a saucer which has been in the freezer or refrigerator.

Put a teaspoon of the conserve on the cold saucer. The conserve should form a slight skin which will wrinkle when you press lightly against it with your index finger.

Published by Murdoch Books® a division of Murdoch Magazines Pty Limited, 45 Jones Street, Ultimo NSW 2007.

Murdoch Books and Le Cordon Bleu thank the 32 masterchefs of all the Le Cordon Bleu Schools, whose knowledge and expertise have made this book possible, especially: Chef Cliche (MOF), Chef Terrien, Chef Boucheret, Chef Duchêne (MOF), Chef Guillut, Chef Steneck, Paris; Chef Males, Chef Walsh, Chef Hardy, London; Chef Chantefort, Chef Bertin, Chef Jambert, Chef Honda, Tokyo; Chef Salembien, Chef Boutin, Chef Harris, Sydney; Chef Lawes, Adelaide; Chef Guiet, Chef Denis, Ottawa. Of the many students who helped the Chefs test each recipe, a special mention to graduates David Welch and Allen Wertheim. A very special acknowledgment to Directors Susan Eckstein, Great Britain, and Kathy Shaw, Paris, who have been responsible for the coordination of the Le Cordon Bleu team throughout this series.

Murdoch Books®
Managing Editor: Kay Halsey
Series Concept, Design and Art Direction: Juliet Cohen
Food Director: Jody Vassallo
Food Editors: Lulu Grimes, Tracy Rutherford
Designer: Annette Fitzgerald
Photographers: Jo Filshie, Chris Jones, Louis Martin
Food Stylists: Carolyn Fienberg, Mary Harris
Food Preparation: Jo Forrest, Alison Turner, Kerrie Mullins
Chef's Techniques Photographer: Reg Morrison
Home Economists: Anna Beaumont, Michelle Lawton, Justine Poole, Kerrie Ray, Margot Smithyman

CEO & Publisher: Anne Wilson
Publishing Director: Catie Ziller
General Manager: Mark Smith
Creative Director: Marylouise Brammer
International Sales Director: Mark Newman

National Library of Australia Cataloguing-in-Publication Data
Breakfasts. ISBN 0 86411 751 5. 1. Breakfasts. (Series: Le Cordon Bleu home collection). 641.52

Printed by Toppan Printing (S) Pte Ltd.
First Printed 1998
©Design and photography Murdoch Books® 1998
©Text Le Cordon Bleu 1998

Distributed in the UK by D Services, 6 Euston Street, Freemen's Common, Leicester LE2 7SS Tel 0116-254-7671 Fax 0116-254-4670. Distributed in Canada by Whitecap (Vancouver) Ltd, 351 Lynn Avenue, North Vancouver, BC V7J 2C4 Tel 604-980-9852 Fax 604-980-8197 or Whitecap (Ontario) Ltd, 47 Coldwater Road, North York, ON M3B 1Y8 Tel 416-444-3442 Fax 416-444-6630

The Publisher and Le Cordon Bleu wish to thank Carole Sweetnam for her help with this series and Villeroy & Boch; Waterford Wedgwood; Le Forge; Home & Garden on The Mall; H.A.G. Import Corp. (Australia) Pty. Ltd. for their assistance in the photography.
Front cover: Brioche, Bagels, Kumquat conserve, Red fruit conserve, French toast with berry compote.

IMPORTANT INFORMATION

CONVERSION GUIDE

1 cup = 250 ml (8 fl oz)
1 Australian tablespoon = 20 ml (4 teaspoons)
1 UK tablespoon = 15 ml (3 teaspoons)

NOTE: We have used 20 ml tablespoons. If you are using a 15 ml tablespoon, for most recipes the difference will be negligible. For recipes using baking powder, gelatine, bicarbonate of soda and flour, add an extra teaspoon for each tablespoon specified.

CUP CONVERSIONS—DRY INGREDIENTS

1 cup flour, plain or self-raising = 125 g (4 oz)
1 cup sugar, caster = 250 g (8 oz)
1 cup breadcrumbs, dry = 125 g (4 oz)

IMPORTANT: Those who might be at risk from the effects of salmonella food poisoning (the elderly, pregnant women, young children and those suffering from immune deficiency diseases) should consult their GP with any concerns about eating raw eggs.